Understanding the Keys to Answer Request

Michael .B. Law

Unless otherwise indicated, all Scripture quotations are from the Holy Bible, *English Standard Version,* @ 2001, 2007, 2011, and 2017 by Crossway, a Good News Publishers publishing ministry. All rights reserved.

UNDERSTANDING THE KEYS TO ANSWER REQUEST

Michael B. Law

P.O. Box 862

Huntsville, Texas

michaelblaw05@gmail.com

Copyright @ 2024 Michael B. Law. All rights reserved. No part of this publication may be reproduced, distributed, or transmitted in any form or by any means, including photocopying, recording, or other electronic or mechanical methods, without the prior written permission of the publisher, except in the case of brief quotations embodied in critical reviews and specific other noncommercial uses permitted by copyright law. For permission requests, write to the publisher,

addressed "Attention: Permissions

Coordinator," at the address below.

ISBN: 978-1-964542-64-5 Paperback

Printed in the United States of America

@2024 by Michael B. Law

Michael B. Law

Understanding The Keys To Answer Request

Front cover image by Artist.

Book design by Designer.

Printed by Amazon Self-Publishing Group in the United States of America.

First printing edition 2024.

Amazon Self-Publishing Group

95 Third Street 2nd Floor San Francisco California 94103 United States of America

Dedication

To my grandmother; you are the reason why I wrote this book. Your sacrifices made it possible for me to achieve my dreams. You are my hero.

To Princess my beloved wife, who fills every moment with love and grace. I appreciate all your support. And my precious daughter, who brings endless joy and light into our world. May the pages of this book reflect the depth of my gratitude and love for you both.

To Susan Baris, thank you for being my greatest supporter and editor; there's no way I could have accomplished the feat of writing this book without you.

To the Amazon Self-Publishing Group; you have changed my life. I am deeply grateful for all the opportunities you gave me. I can't wait to continue to impact lives with you. The best is yet to come.

Foreword

In a world filled with challenges and uncertainties, the journey of faith often feels like traversing an uncharted path. As believers, we yearn for guidance and assurance, seeking tools that will help us navigate through life's trials and tribulations. Michael B. Law's ***"Understanding the Keys to Answer Request"*** serves as a comprehensive guide, illuminating the path to a deeper, more fulfilling relationship with God.

This book is a testament to the power of faith and the profound impact it can have on our lives. Michael B. Law draws from the wellspring of his spiritual journey, offering readers a treasure trove of insights and practical tools that have been instrumental in his walk with God. His dedication to exploring and mastering these tools is evident in every chapter, providing a clear roadmap for believers to follow.

"Understanding the Keys to Answer Request" delves into the essential elements of faith, including the power of God's Word, the significance of thanksgiving and praise, the transformative potential of prayer, the spiritual discipline of fasting, the blessings of giving, and the imperative of evangelism. Each chapter is meticulously crafted to offer not only theoretical knowledge but also practical applications that can be seamlessly integrated into daily life.

One of the standout features of this book is its emphasis on the intentional use of faith tools. Michael B. Law encourages readers to approach their relationship with God with purpose and dedication, recognizing that faith is not a passive experience but an active, dynamic journey. By mastering these tools, believers can unlock the full potential of their faith, experiencing divine intervention and transformation in every aspect of their lives.

The power of God's Word is the cornerstone of this book, reflecting the belief that Scripture is a living, breathing testament of God's promises. Michael B. Law illustrates how immersing oneself in the Bible can bring clarity, strength, and direction. He provides practical advice on how to study and meditate on the Word, allowing it to become a source of daily inspiration and guidance.

Thanksgiving and praise are highlighted as vital practices that shift our focus from our problems to the greatness of God. Michael B. Law emphasizes that a heart full of gratitude opens doors to divine blessings and peace. Through personal anecdotes and biblical examples, he demonstrates how cultivating a spirit of thankfulness can transform our outlook and attract God's favor.

Prayer, described as the lifeline of faith, is another critical tool explored in this book. Michael B. Law provides deep insights into different types of prayers, from supplication to intercession, and the importance of praying with faith and expectation. He shares powerful testimonies of answered prayers, encouraging readers to develop a robust and consistent prayer life.

The discipline of fasting, often misunderstood or neglected, is presented with clarity and purpose. Michael B. Law explains the spiritual benefits of fasting, from breaking strongholds to gaining spiritual clarity. He offers practical guidelines on how to fast effectively, ensuring that readers understand both the physical and spiritual aspects of this powerful practice.

Giving, an expression of love and obedience, is another key focus of this book. Michael B. Law delves into the principles of tithing and generous giving, highlighting the joy and blessings that come from a heart willing to share. He provides biblical insights and personal experiences that illustrate the impact of giving on both the giver and the recipient.

Evangelism, the calling to share the Good News, is presented as an essential tool for every believer. Michael B. Law encourages readers to embrace the Great Commission, offering practical strategies for witnessing and sharing their faith with others. He underscores the importance of living a life that reflects God's love, making evangelism a natural and impactful part of daily life.

This foreword would be incomplete without acknowledging the reflective dedication and love that Michael B. Law has poured into this work. His heartfelt dedication to his grandmother, wife, daughter, and all those who have supported him is a testament to the power of love and gratitude in shaping our spiritual journey. It is a reminder that the journey of faith is not a solitary one but is enriched by the relationships and support of those around us.

Michael B. Law's personal journey is woven throughout the book, providing a relatable and inspiring narrative that encourages readers to persevere in their own faith journey. His transparency and authenticity make ***"Understanding the Keys to Answer Request"*** not just a manual but a companion for anyone seeking to deepen their relationship with God.

As you embark on this journey through ***"Understanding the Keys to Answer Request,"*** may you find inspiration, guidance, and a renewed sense of purpose. Let this book be a beacon of light, guiding you towards a deeper understanding of God's love and the incredible power of faith. May it equip you with the tools you need to navigate life's challenges and emerge victorious, knowing that with God, all things are possible.

Michael B. Law has given us a gift—a key to unlocking the divine. It is now up to us to take this key, master these tools, and step into the fullness of our faith. Let us embrace this journey with open hearts and minds, ready to experience the transformative power of a life lived in close communion with God.

God bless,
Ethel Kenneth John
Senior Editor

About the Author

Michael B. Law is a licensed minister and a criminal justice expert in the United States. Over 23 years in Apostolic-prophetic mandates have reached and transformed lives across diverse nations. Dedicated to his mission, Michael combines his profound understanding of criminal justice with his spiritual insights to offer guidance and support to those in need.

When he's not busy with his ministerial duties or criminal justice work, Michael cherishes spending time with his family. His passion is helping Christians understand and develop a deeper relationship with God, inspiring many to walk in faith and purpose.

Contents

Introduction 1
One 4
    His Word 4
    In His Image 7
    By His Word 8
Two Thanksgiving 10
Three Praise 15
    The Highway of Praise 16
Four Prayer 22
    Prophetic Prayer 23
    General Principles 24
Five Evangelism 30
    Heavens Favorites 31
    Divine Increase 31
    Divine Promotion 33
    Evangelistic 34
    Open Doors 35
Six Fasting 36
    The Fast Lane 38
    The Believer's Vocation 39
    Types of Fasting 39
    Esther Fast: 39

Samuel Fast 39

Elijah Fast: 39

Ezra Fast: 39

Daniel Fast: 40

John the Baptist Fast: 40

Jesus Fast: 40

How to Fast 40

Normal Fast: 40

Partial Fast: 40

Absolute Fast: 40

SEVEN GIVING 42

Acceptable Sacrifice 43

The Glorious Lifestyle 43

1 Firstfruits 43

The Mystery of Increase 44

2 Tithe 45

3 Sacrificial Offering 45

CONCLUSION 48

INTRODUCTION

Many people have given up on God because of no solution to their needs. Some hoped for changes, which never happened. Do we blame God? NO! They failed to discover the tools to communicate with God. The cars and houses Christians pray for as needs are not prayers to unbelievers. But believers fail to realize we must understand how to approach God with our requests using His Word as a parameter. God will grant needs at the right time as aligns with His Word. *"For you have exalted above all things your name and your Word"* (**Ps. 138:2c**).

Our God is loving; we expect this from Him, who lives according to His rules and keeps His promises. That is why we have faith in Him but not in man. We cannot ask for a better God or a better example.

However, the mighty God is not a respecter of persons. He will not save a man because he is a Jew, or because he is rich, or educated, or of lofty rank, or on account of external rights. He allows everyone to receive the blessings available by the plan of salvation, irrespective of who we are. *But we* are all saved by adoption in Christ. Peter said, *"Truly I understand that God shows no partiality"* (**Acts 10:34b**).

Research has revealed there are more than 4,300 religions worldwide. Christianity, Islam, Judaism, Hinduism, and Buddhism are the most prevalent. Christians are mandated to pray without ceasing. Muslims pray five times daily. Jews pray morning, afternoon, and evening. While Hindus perform rituals three times daily, Buddhists pray three times, which is equal to the Jewish pattern. These various religions have processes of worship with results.

The fundamental question is: Why do Christians pray with no results? Folks, candidly, our intention matters when we come before God. If our identity is in Christ, the heart's intentions will align with the Word of God regarding righteousness, and we will get the answer to our request.

But suppose our identity is in the love of self. In that case, the intentions of our heart will seek personal pleasure without regard to the consequences that derive from it. *James 4.3 says,* "You ask and do not receive, because you ask wrongly, to spend it on your passions."

God rewards and responds when the heart is correct, and the proper tool is in use. *"Knowing that whatever good anyone does, this he will receive back from the Lord, whether he is a bondservant or is free"* **(Eph. 6:8)**.

God detests ignorance, which can have adverse effects on anyone and societies at large. For example, scientific ignorance offers the opportunity to seek knowledge and make discoveries by asking new questions.

Likewise, God wants us to benefit by desiring to learn His ways. Therefore, it is vital to search and find the right tools to communicate with God to forge ahead. As the Bible says, *"It is the glory of God to conceal a thing: but the honors of kings are to search out a matter"* ***(Prov. 25:2).***

God promises to give keys to those who ask: *"I will give unto the keys of the kingdom of heaven, and whatever you bind on earth shall be bound in heaven, and whatever you loose on earth shall be loosed in heaven"* (***Matt. 16:19***). Folks, you have the key. Still, you must act in obedience according to His will.

So, come as we unravel those tools of asking and receiving through the guidance of the Holy Spirit to get answers to our requests. *"Likewise, the Spirit helps us in our weakness. We do not know what to pray for as we ought, but the Spirit intercedes for us with groanings too deep for words. And he who searches hearts knows what is the mind of the Spirit because the Spirit intercedes for the saints according to the will of God"* ***(Rom. 8: 26-27).***

Friends, we need the Holy Spirit to teach us how to approach God using His word, thanksgiving, praise, prayer, fasting, giving, and evangelism as tools. And once we master them, we will experience answers to our requests.

ONE

Someone is reading this book because he needs an answer to a life question. The methods God revealed that are captured in this book can handle the challenges of life, family, ministry, and business. Suppose you apply this information to your situation. Closed doors can open, mountains will skip, what seems impossible, shall become possible, and we shall reign in life through Christ.

God never created us to be victims of circumstances. He started us as conquerors and overcomers in this world. It is customary for thieves to use master keys to break into people's property, regardless of the type of doors, cars, or other gadgets. The master key can open any door.

The Bible contains secret keys, and this book reveals the tools needed to open closed doors. The Word of God is a master key that opens doors. God created everything and man through the instrumentality of His Word.

HIS WORD

God's Word is a secret code that brought the world into reality. His Word is the master key that unlocks closed doors, unravels the mystery, undoes every deleted item, and restores life to its original purpose. God's Word is not literature. His Word is more powerful than the most explosive dynamite. It is active, it preserves, and it can control the most ruthless, contrary wind.

And a great windstorm arose, and the waves were breaking into the boat so that the boat was already filling. But he was in the stern, asleep on the cushion. And they woke him and said to him, "Teacher, do you not care that we are perishing? And he awoke, rebuked the wind, and said to the sea, "Peace! Be still!" And the wind ceased, and there was a great calm.
Mark 4:37 39

The disturbances of life are stormy. They come upon us, frighten us, and threaten to destroy all our stability and safety. We wonder if we'll survive them. We wonder how long they will last. At least, that's how a storm at sea would be for most of us. For Jesus, this was but an occasion to wink.

Storms—don't worry! Jesus is with us while they're here, but He's perfectly calm over them. He's not afraid or anxious. For us, He seems to sleep on a switch. We wonder why He does not stand up and do something. Does He even know we are in trouble? We don't know how much He cares. Whether He even can do anything about it. Whether He's all, He's cracked up to be.

This generation has yet to discover and retain the Word's power. No situation can defy God's Word. *"As for God, his way is perfect: the word of the Lord is tried: he is a buckler to all those that trust in him"* ***(Ps. 18:30)***. His Word works with dispatch. It is laden with uncommon power and can penetrate every aspect of life. *"For the word of God is quick, powerful, and sharper than any two-edged sword, piercing even to the dividing asunder of soul and spirit, and of the joints and marrow, and is a discerner of the thoughts and intents of the heart"* (**Heb. 4:12**). While we are still in this world other than our heavenly home, God's Word is alive and active, sharper than any double-edged sword. God's Word never stops penetrating the separation of soul and spirit on this earthly journey to our heavenly home.

The Word never fails to distinguish between good and evil, God and the world, faith and fear, and what is Christ and what is not. So, discovering the power in His Word validates our authority to exercise dominion over all challenges of life creation. *"Through faith, we understand that the worlds were framed by the Word of God so that things which are seen were not made of things which do appear"* (**Heb. 11:3**). "It is evident that God's Word is a tool to open heaven. The Word of God is powerful, constant, and yes, amen" (**2 Cor. 1:20**).

In creation, God never sourced materials or looked for labor. He spoke the Word of faith that brought forth His desires.

In the beginning, God created the heavens and the earth. The earth was without form and void, and darkness was over the face of the deep. And the Spirit of God was hovering over the face of the waters. And God said, "Let there be light," and there was light. Genesis 1:1-3

God did a lot in creation, yet the things we see today were never in place at the beginning. God rearranged everything by the word of His mouth. *"Through faith, we understand that the worlds were framed by the word of God so that things which are seen were not made of things which do appear" (Heb. 11:3).*

IN HIS IMAGE

God formed man and placed him in charge of all creation. Genesis 1:25 records: *"Then God said, 'Let us make man in our image, after our likeness. And let them have dominion over the fish of the sea and over the birds of the heavens and over the livestock and over all the earth and over every creeping thing that creeps on the earth.'"*

Man has the power to do whatever he imagines because he is the god on the planet. *"I said, 'You are gods, sons of the Most High, all of you'" (Ps. 82:6).* This use of the word **"gods"** about humans is rare, but it is found elsewhere in the Old Testament. For example, when God sent Moses to Pharaoh, God said, *"Behold, I have made you god unto Pharaoh" (Exod. 7:1).* It means Moses spoke God's word as God's messenger and thus became God's agent to the king.

God's Word is the standard to receive anything. Answers to life's issues are in the meditation of the word of God. The psalmist declares, *"Let the words of my mouth and the meditation of my heart be acceptable in your sight, O Lord, my rock and my redeemer" (Ps. 19:14).*

Jesus did mighty works in His earthly ministry because He was a student of the Word. *"And it came to pass, that after three days they found him in the temple, sitting in the midst of the doctors, both hearing them and asking them questions" (Luke 2:46).* His miracle in John 2, when He changed the water into wine, was through the instrumentality of the spoken word.

BY HIS WORD

The miracles Jesus performed in the Bible were through the power of the spoken Word. The blind eyes made open, the deaf ears healed, and the lame who walked were all done through the spoken Word. Folks, if we are willing to use the Word as a tool whenever needed and be obedient to the Holy Spirit, God's words will do wonders. "Death and life are in the power of the tongue: and they that love it shall eat the fruit thereof" (Prov. 18:21).

God's Word is paramount to life, family, ministry, business, marriage, finance, and much more. We must meditate on God's Word to receive heaven's touch. *"This book of the law shall not depart out of thy mouth, but thou shalt meditate therein day and night, that thou mayest observe to do according to all that is written therein: for then thou shalt make thy way prosperous, and then thou shalt have good success"* (***Josh. 1:8***). God also promised, "So shall my word be that goes forth from my mouth, it shall not return to me void but shall accomplish what I please, and it shall prosper in the thing for which I sent it" (Isa. 55:11).

Friend, there is a word for you in God's Word. Please stand up, discover it, apply it to your circumstances, and expect a turnaround. We must trust God's Word and speak it to accomplish our desires. We need to use God's Word as a therapy for our situations. He will grant our hearts' desires.

Friends, God created everything and man through the instrumentality of His Word. God's Word is paramount to life, family, business, ministry, and more. We must meditate on God's Word to receive heaven's touch. Indeed, there is no gainsaying there is power in His Word. It is the master key and the standard to receive anything.

Two

Thanksgiving

The Bible contains secret keys that can open doors. Thanksgiving might be a key needed to replace long prayers in some situations. Its effectiveness is yet to be discovered by Christian believers. When we approach God with a grateful heart, it prepares the ground for a new miracle. As Paul says, *"Give thanks in all circumstances; for this is the will of God in Christ Jesus for you" (1 Thess. 5:18).*

Life comes with challenges. Many wear long faces while multitudes grumble and complain of unpleasant predicaments. It is not uncommon to roll our eyes or murmur and recite a litany of woes, tragedies, and mishaps. But those who remain thankful stay on top. Folks, lots of problems linger due to the lack of thanksgiving. Paul calls upon his readers to be grateful under all circumstances. He adds that this is the will of God, no matter how complex our cases may be.

Christians are on the dark side of life today due to ungratefulness. They should appreciate God for the sunshine He beams over them. Instead, they choose to commit suicide for not having money, a marriage, children, or shelter. However, if they use thanksgiving, it can change obstacles to miracles and sadness to happiness. Peter promises, *"And after you have suffered a little while, the God of all grace, who has called you to his eternal glory in Christ, will himself restore, confirm, strengthen, and establish you"* **(1 Peter 5:10)**.

The above scripture was the consolation that kept me going. Friends, suffering in this life will occur, but it will end for those who believe in Christ. Not only this, believers will be "restored" from all the evil done to us. In my early days of ministry, I was homeless, with only two pairs of trousers and shirts. There was usually no food, so I had to scour for food. Indeed, it was a bitter experience, but I understood God's plans, so I remained resolute. I faced ridicule as a college graduate who failed to work. Family and friends saw an unserious young man, but I saw a great future.

Folks, it is good to thank God in every situation. As 1 **Thessalonians 5:18** says, *"Give thanks in all circumstances; for this is the will of God in Christ Jesus for you."* God can lift anyone from zero to hero, from nobody to somebody, from shame to fame, from nothing to something. I have witnessed God's favor in places and corridors of power through the power of thanksgiving.

In August 2002, I was praying and fasting in a prayer camp. One morning, as I set out for prayer, the Holy Spirit whispered, "Thank the Lord!" I obeyed, and He then spoke, "I have heard your request." Behold, that week, God opened international doors for global ministry.

Friend, stop the devil from denying you God's blessing. Rise and give thanks and see problems become promotions. Trust me, thanksgiving is a vital tool for communicating with God.

Psalm 100:4a says, *"Enter his gates with thanksgiving."* David identified a gate and broke through it with the tool of thanksgiving. He said, *"Lift up your heads, O ye gates; even lift up them, ye everlasting doors; and the King of glory shall come in"* ***(Ps. 24:9)***.

There are gates that were in existence before you were born. They were there even before your fathers were born, and each door has a gatekeeper. These gates are erected to prevent us from reaching our goal. Folks, we need the correct access code or key to open them.

David reveals to us a thanksgiving weapon to free God's people from bondage. So, before you declare days of fasting and prayer just as I did, ask the Holy Spirit because your case might require the tool of thanksgiving.

Abel offered a sacrifice of thanks unto God: *"By faith, Abel offered to God a more acceptable sacrifice than Cain, through which he was commended as righteous, God commending him by accepting his gifts"* ***(Heb. 11:4)***. God responded with fire from the heavens, and His blessing came to him. When we have faith in God and live a faithful life, it results in thanksgiving and praise to God.

Unfortunately, the thanksgiving we bring to God is often superficial. Often, our motives for praising God are not pure. Much debate has happened over why God accepted Abel's offering and not Cain's. The most common idea is that Abel's offering was the proper sacrifice.

In Genesis 4, there is an argument that Cain and Abel's sacrifice was an offering of sin. But reflecting on it, there is no indication that the offering was an offering for sin. The offerings of Cain and Abel were offerings of thanksgiving rather than offerings for sin. The issue here is motive and heart, not the actual sacrifice itself.

How often do we go to church and sing hymns of praise while, at the same time, our minds are preoccupied with other things? How often do we sing songs of praise without any attention given to the words we are singing? How often do we go through the motions of worship rather than worshiping God in spirit and truth? I see it all the time.

Also, the Lord Jesus Christ used the thanksgiving tool to bring Lazarus back to life. Before Christ came, the whole city had gathered to see what He could do. Lazarus died after four days and was buried. *"Then they removed the stone from where the dead was laid. So they took away the stone. And Jesus lifted up his eyes and said, "Father, I thank you that you have heard me"* ***(John 11:41)***. Lazarus returned to life, and those gathered left the scene in shame. Folks, some people might predict your failure and not see any good things in what you do. God is not like them. He promised, *"If anyone stirs up strife, it is not from me; whoever stirs up strife with you shall fall because of you" (**Isa. 54:15**)*. I pray that all who have mocked you shall fail.

Christians lack these results due to a lack of communion with the Holy Spirit. Nothing is more horrible than a hopeless situation. We must approach God with a grateful heart for Him to prepare new ground for us. Complaining about unpleasant predicaments and challenges, wearing long faces, and grumbling will take us nowhere. Paul calls upon his readers to be thankful in all situations. He adds that this is the will of God.

Folks, I have faced ordeals of life, and these thanksgiving tools that I applied gave me victory. So, stop the devil from denying God's blessing. Rise and give thanks, no matter how complicated your case may be. Trust me, my friend, thanksgiving is vital for communicating with God. Through it, you will see your problems turn into promotions.

THREE

PRAISE

Praise is another powerful tool in communicating with God. Musicians have mastered the art of praise. Praise singers in some cultures have demonstrated the ability to make people empty their pockets in response to praise and adoration. How much more if we praise God in our situations?

David said he would "enter God's courts with praise" *(Ps. 100:4)*. The psalmist opened his chorus by inviting the other worshippers to share his excitement and joyful euphoria: *"Make a joyful noise to the Lord, all the world! Give joy to the Lord! Come to his presence with the song!" (Psalm 100:1-2)*

Dear friends, we must rejoice, serve, sing, study, grace, praise, and bless His name because the Lord is good, His love remains forever, and He is faithful. God takes delight in praise. What He does in response to the praises of His children has surprised both young and old believers. Praise has worked where other methods have failed.

Praise draws power from heaven, unfolds God's compassion, attracts His favor, and draws a cord from our heavenly Father's gracious heart. We can praise our way to a breakthrough.

THE HIGHWAY OF PRAISE

Praise gladdens God's heart and makes the devil mad. The devil hates seeing a child of God lost in the splendor of praise. The shortest route to procuring divine pleasure is the highway of praise.

We may ask, what is praise? Praise is an expression that centers on celebrating God's attitude, worshiping His majesty, and extolling His name. Since God is greater and *more affluent, He deserves our highest praise. The Bible says, "Yet you are holy, enthroned on the praises of Israel"* (**Ps. 22:3**). Praise is a way of honoring or paying homage to God.

When a believer becomes a praise addict, God will be pleased to bless him. David, "A man after my God's heart," used the weapon and tool of praise to defeat Satan: *"The Lord has sought out a man after his own heart, and the Lord has commanded him to be prince"* (**1 Sam. 13:14b**). David faced many battles in life, but in all the wars, he was victorious because he used his tool of praise.

Moses and the children of Israel understood the power of praise to bring down His presence in the wilderness. *"Who is like unto thee, O Lord, among all the other gods? Who is like thee glorious in holiness, fearful in praises, doing wonders?"* (**Exod. 15:11**).

The wonders in David's life were by the tools of praise. He defeated Saul because whenever evil spirits came upon Saul,

David used the power of praise to cast out the demons. *"And it came to pass, when the evil Spirit from God was upon Saul, that David took a harp, and played with his hand: so, Saul was refreshed and was well, and the evil Spirit departed from him" (1 Sam. 16:23).*

Demons hate praises; I notice this each time I conduct deliverance prayers. The Holy Spirit leads me into praises, and the stubborn demons bow instantaneously.

Deborah, a prophetess and the wife of Lapidoth, judged Israel for a time and faced battles (***Judges 4***: end). The Lord gave victory to Israel, and they praised the Lord.

On that day, Deborah and Barak, son of Abinoam, sang this song: When the princes in Israel take the lead, and the people willing to offer themselves—*praise the Lord! Hear this, you kings! Listen, you rulers! I, even I, will sing to the Lord; I will praise the Lord, the God of Israel, in song.* **Judges 5:1-3**

If you want to defeat the enemies, praise. If you wish to rest, praise God. Honestly, it is a potent tool that can unlock the floodgates of heaven. However, remember this was the duty of Lucifer in heaven before he lost it due to pride. *"How you are fallen from heaven O Day Star, son of Dawn! How you are cut down to the ground, you who laid the nations low!!"* **(Isa. 14:12).** *"You were an anointed guardian cherub. I placed you; you were on the holy mountain of God; in the midst of the stones of fire, you* *walked. You were blameless in your ways from the day you were created, till unrighteousness was found in you"* **(Ezek. 28:14-15)**.

Among the seven sins God hates the most, pride is at the head of the list. There are six things the Lord hates; seven are abominations to Him:

Haughty eyes, a lying tongue, and hands that shed innocent blood, a heart that devises wicked plans, feet that make haste to run to evil, a false witness who breathes out lies, and one who sows discord among brothers. **Proverbs 6:16-19**

When you look at that list, you can see that Satan (even before or just in Genesis 3) reveals every one of those virtues:

- haughty eyes: "I will make myself the Most High."

- a lying tongue: "said God?"

- shedding innocent blood (he knew God would chastise Adam and Eve with immediate separation from Him as well as mortality leading to ultimate death)

- a heart that devises the wicked plans (of man's fall)

- feet that make haste to run to evil (reasonably within a few days after day seven of creation week)

- a false witness who breathes out lies (perjury against God's own words) and who sows discord among angels in heaven

However, in Hebrew 13:15, the Bible says, *"By him, therefore, let us offer the sacrifice of praise to God continually, that is, the fruit of our lips giving thanks to his name."* Praise is a meal to God; it quenches God's hunger. And praise should not be only in the sanctuary but anytime, anywhere, and always. I love the way David put it in Psalm 119:164, *"Seven times a day, I praise thee because of thy righteous judgment."* If you want the judgment of God over your case, praise God.

We must adopt the power of praise as our nature in Christ. *"Wilt thou show wonders to the dead? Shall the dead arise and praise thee?" (Ps. 88:10).* Here, David affirms that praise can bring dead things back to life.

In 2 Chronicle 20:1, something extraordinary happened in the life of King Jehoshaphat. The Moabites and Ammonites came into battle with the children of Israel. The Moabites and the Ammonites were descendants of the children born to Lot by his two daughters (***Gen. 19:33-38***). Lot was Abraham's nephew. Invariably, the Moabites and Ammonites were Israel's cousins.

Jehoshaphat became fearful because of the Moabites' strength and the Ammonites' strength. King Jehoshaphat proclaimed fasting throughout the land. Fasting is one of the secret tools that can open the heavens. We will elaborate more on fasting in other chapters. The people fasted but were still very afraid. The king was reminded of God's awesomeness and testimonies to Israel, but God still did not speak. *"Your testimonies are my heritage forever, for they are the joy of my heart" (Psalm 119:111).*

The king became troubled because God was silent. Why? Because the right tool for the battle was not being used. Something unique happened in 2 Chronicle 20:13-21. The Israelites gathered their families and looked up to God. While waiting, the Spirit of the Lord came upon Jahaziel, a Levite. He spoke: *"Hearken ye, all Judah, and ye inhabitant of Jerusalem, and thou king Jehoshaphat, thus saith the Lord unto you, 'Be not afraid nor dismayed because of this great multitude, for the battle is not yours, but God's'"* **(2 Chron. 20:15)**. As God's Spirit spoke through Jahaziel, he led Israel into praise. Immediately, the Lord took control of the battle, and all the enemies died.

Are you murmuring or complaining? It is time to stand up and kick out the devil in praising the Lord. The devil lost his position in heaven, but trust me, God is committed to your case. So, honor God in praise and be blessed.

God takes delight in praise in our situations. He wants to see us rejoice, serve, sing, study, grace, praise, and bless His name. Praise draws power from heaven, gladdens God's heart, and makes the devil mad. When we are addicted to praise, God will be pleased to bless us.

Moses and the children of Israel understood the power of praise to bring down His presence in the wilderness. David, a man after my God's heart, used the weapon of praise to defeat the devil in all situations. Also, Deborah, a prophetess and the wife of Lapidoth, used the same key of praise to lead Israel to victory in battle. We can see, therefore, that there is no controversy over the power of praise if we must defeat the enemy. So, get up! It is time to kick the devil out by praising God.

FOUR

PRAYER

Prayer is a tool to secure breakthroughs in life. To open the doors of our breakthroughs, we need prayer to unfold God's purpose and plan for our lives. Prayer generates power for the future.

However, prayer goes beyond asking and receiving. Through prayer, we can speak to God and hear from Him. In my walk with God, I have discovered that prayer is broad and varies. For prayer to be effective, it must come from the groaning of the Holy Spirit with prophetic insight into the will of God.

Prayer can inspire, encourage, and uplift as God speaks to us. It gives us predictive insights into what He intends to do in any situation. Also, it is a dialogue between God and man. We get assurances and words of hope when we pray, and prayer becomes more pleasurable. *"O you who hear prayer, to you shall all flesh come"* **(Ps. 65:2)**.

*"Likewise, the Spirit helps us in our weakness. We do not know what to pray for as we ought, but the Spirit intercedes for us with groanings too deep for words. And he who searches hearts knows what is the mind of the Spirit because the Spirit intercedes for the saints according to the will of God"***(Rom. 8:26-27)***. This verse is

the bedrock of approaching God mixed with faith. The Holy Spirit wants our communion as we listen to His voice in all circumstances.

PROPHETIC PRAYER

Prayer has become an exciting experience for me. I have seen God even manifest His power through prayer offered over the phone. Prayer can be a great experience, and be willing to pray when God decks your prayers with a crown of testimonies. I have seen God perform great miracles in response to prophetic prayers.

So, what is prophetic prayer?

Prophetic prayer is praying scripturally in faith through the guidance of the Holy Spirit. During a trip, I saw God perform an outstanding miracle during a church service in New York. Prophetic words came forth to a lady with problems with her menstrual cycle. A few days later, she returned rejoicing, for her menstruation came at age forty-four—a fantastic miracle.

A sister became apprehensive because she discovered lumps in her breast. She was so scared of breast cancer, and she thought the end had come. She received a prophetic word and was healed. The lumps disappeared, and thoughts of cancer vanished.

God demonstrated the power of prophetic prayer in a crusade in Accra, Ghana, in August 2003. The Holy Spirit spoke to me: "Someone is here, born deaf and dumb." An eight-year-old girl came to the podium for prayers; she was healed and began to hear and speak, and the crowd rejoiced. *"Truly, truly, I say to you, whoever believes in me will also do the works that I do; and greater works than these will he do, because I am going to the Father"* **(John 14:12)**.

GENERAL PRINCIPLES

There are general principles of prayer. Prayer is one tool for communicating with God to secure breakthroughs. Prayer is not a monologue but a dialogue, and God speaks as we pray. Prayer is vital because man has been offering prayers to God since creation, and we cannot be an exception.

There are books on prayers, but this masterpiece explains prayer as one of the tools used in communicating with God. It offers practical solutions for the quest of many unanswered requests.

Prayer may be more complex than we think. Jesus's disciples faced the challenge of casting out the spirit of madness from a young man. They prayed, just like any of us, but without a solution. The boy was brought to Jesus for prayers and was healed instantaneously. The disciples were amazed. They asked Jesus why they could not heal the boy. He answered, *"Howbeit this kind goeth not out but by prayer and fasting"* **(Matt. 17:21)**.

Prayer and fasting are tools used in communicating with God. Jesus taught His disciples how to pray. *"And it came to pass that, as he was praying in a certain place when he ceased, one of his disciples said unto him, Lord, teach us to pray, as John also taught his disciples"* (**Luke 11:1**).

Prayer is deep. Jesus prayed in different places and diverse patterns. He prayed in the wilderness, cities, seaside, mountains, garden, cross, and by the tomb. He prayed in the wilderness after being baptized by John. He was led through the Holy Spirit to be tempted by the devil. He fasted forty days and nights in the wilderness. *"Then Jesus was led up by the Spirit into the wilderness to be tempted by the devil"* (**Matt. 4:1**).

Things may be difficult, but we can always trust God. To believe in God in the desert is to turn to God in prayer, not far from Him in silence, which means turning to God to be fed spiritually in every situation.

Also, the prophets in the Bible prayed in different ways and places by the leading of the Spirit. Examples are Jonah, Elijah, Daniel, etc. Jonah prayed from the inside of the fish unto God. He said, *"In my distress, I called the Lord, and he responded. I asked for help deep in the tomb, and you heard my cry* (**Jonah 2:2**).

Today, how many Christians practice the same pattern of prayer? Are we not obliged to do the same? Of course, we are! *"The former treatise have I made, O Theophilus, of all that Jesus* *began both to do and teach, Until the day in which he was taken up, after that he through the Holy Ghost had given commandments unto the apostles whom he had chosen" (**Acts 1:1-2**).*

Folks, we need to master these tools for effective communication with God through Christ. There are gates in heaven, and we need the right tools to gain access. Jacob said, *"How dreadful this place is, this is none other but the house of God, and this is the gate of heaven"* (**Gen. 28:17**).

Jacob wrestled with an angel. He understood God's will and deployed the strategic warfare tool. He wrestled, and God changed his name from Jacob to Israel. We need the Holy Spirit to help our infirmity as we come before God with our requests.

In 2 Chronicles 7, Solomon offered a sacrifice of prayer unto God after the Temple's completion. God appeared to him at night, saying He had answered his prayers and had chosen the place for Himself as a meeting point between them. Some prayers are to be in a specific location. If not, there will be no response. At times, God needs a consecrated place and time to meet with us.

As seen in Mark 1:35, Jesus had the habit of rising early to pray in a solitary place. If prayer is a tool, we must dedicate a place and time to meet with God. If Christ did it, we are obliged as His followers to do the same: "The disciple is not above his master: but everyone perfect shall be his master (***Luke 6:40***). Also, for our prayers to be accepted, we must confess and repent from our sins:

"If I regard iniquity in my heart, the lord will not hear me" (**Ps. 66:18**). God's eyes cannot behold evil, and a sinner's prayer is an abomination before Him. Once we confess and repent genuinely, His grace will be more than sufficient again.

James 5:16-18 says, *"The effectual fervent prayer of a righteous man availeth much." Elias was a man subject to like passions; he prayed earnestly that it might not rain, and it rained not on the earth for three years and six months. And he prayed again, and the heaven gave rain, and the earth brought forth her fruit."*

The God we serve is no respecter of any man; His principles remain the same. Elijah was a man like us. He prayed, and heaven honored his word. *"Call unto me, and I will answer thee, and shew thee great and mighty things, which thou knowest not"* (***Jer. 33:3***). Folks, there is no magic with God once we obey His law.

Peradventure, we live righteously and have repented from our sins, but it seems there is no answer to our prayers. At times, the answers are immediate, and when delayed, God wants to see us manifest the right characters and fruits of the Spirit to avoid His name being dragged in the mud after we receive the blessing. *"But the fruit of the Spirit is love, joy, peace, longsuffering, gentleness, goodness, faith, meekness, temperance: against such there is no law"* (***Gal. 5:22-23***).

All the more so, our God is the master of the universe; He decides what is best for us. *"Behold, I am the Lord, the God of all flesh: is there anything too hard for me?"* **(Jer. 32:27)**.

The armed robber on the cross received immediate forgiveness because he found mercy. Hannah prayed for years before she got an answer.

Years ago, as a young believer, I lived in a shared apartment but kept praying to God concerning my accommodations. Each time I prayed; the Lord assured me of an apartment. It was terrible that I had to move to a cheap guest house in town. I gathered money for the mini apartment, and on my way to pay, God spoke to a ministry partner to offer me an apartment. She took care of the payment for a furnished, two-bedroom apartment for three years. God answered! It took time, but He beautified His name in His time.

Honestly, prayer is a means to secure breakthroughs in life. It unfolds God's purpose and generates power for the future. However, we must understand prayer goes beyond asking and receiving. It is not a monologue but a dialogue, and God speaks as we pray. To see the results of our prayers, we must understand the groaning of the Holy Spirit with a prophetic insight into God's will in any situation.

Prayer is strategic, and Jesus taught His disciples how to pray at different times and places. Likewise, prophets in the Bible prayed in various ways and places by the leading of the Spirit. Examples are Jonah, Elijah, and Daniel. Also, in this chapter, we witnessed the diverse testimonies of people who prayed, not excluding me.

God is no respecter of any man, and principles remain the same. There is no magic once we obey God's laws and approach Him with the correct key. Apply these principles, and your problems and challenges will vanish. The Bible says in ***Ecclesiastes 7:8***, *"Better is the ending of a thing than the beginning thereof: and the patient in Spirit is better than the proud in spirit."* Friends, continue to build up yourself, believe in God, and He will grant your request.

Five

Evangelism

The coming of the Lord hinges on the evangelization of the lost. To bring back Christ, the King, we must evangelize. Evangelism is the heartbeat of God. Involvement with evangelism, be it mass or personal evangelism, is one tool that will open the door to breakthroughs and miracles.

We don't have to coerce God into granting our heart's desires before He gives us a blessing. If we are involved in evangelizing the lost and reaching the unreached, the Lord will be busy taking care of our concerns.

If the Bible can state there is joy in heaven over every soul who repents, then evangelism must mean much to God. *Luke 15:7* says, *"I say unto you that likewise, joy shall be in Heaven over one sinner that repenteth, more than ninety and nine just persons, which need no repentance."* If this is true, evangelism is one of the master tools that opens all doors. It is one unique tool that opens the windows of heaven fast. Since God does not want one soul to perish, He will do everything possible to grant us open doors in every area of life.

HEAVENS FAVORITES

Those busy carrying out soul-winning efforts will always remain heaven's favorites. Any believer who aims to see the lost saved will be highly favored. *"The fruit of the righteous is a tree of life, and he that winneth souls are wise. Behold, the righteous shall be recompensed in the earth: much more the wicked and the sinner"* (***Prov. 11:30-31***).

The righteous believer who gets involved with evangelism shall receive great rewards. God lavishes His love and care upon His children who are busy winning souls. God will do anything to show His pleasure in the lives of His servants.

Let us examine things from a secular angle. Organizations generally invest enormous resources in staff members who contribute immensely towards the organization's overall progress. Management decisions are taken concerning staff training to make them offer their best to the organization.

DIVINE INCREASE

From my experience, God takes delight in granting excellent opportunities to men and women who are busy advancing His kingdom on earth. God expects you to invest your resources, time, and energy in soul-winning. He wants you to go from house to house, from one city to another, declaring the kingdom's gospel. If your most significant focus on earth is evangelism, God will turn on the searchlight of favor upon you. When you invest your resources in soul-winning, God continues to increase your resources.

I have learned God generally releases more grace to those addicted to evangelism. As you speak, the gifts and blessings of the Holy Spirit impart to the lost. In my personal experience, I have discovered and received great favor as I have evangelized. *"And with great power gave the apostles witness of the resurrection of the Lord Jesus: and great grace was upon them"* (**Acts 4:33**).

"God bearing them witness, both with signs and wonders, and with diver's miracles, and gifts of the Holy Ghost according to his own will" (**Heb. 2:4**).

God has led me into what I describe as prophetic evangelism. It is preaching through the instrumentality of the Spirit of prophecy. Many would never listen to the gospel without demonstrating the gifts of the Holy Spirit: discernment, interpretation of tongues, word of knowledge, wisdom, and prophecy. The lost want reasons to believe in the gospel of Christ: *"Then said Jesus unto him, except you see signs and wonders, ye will not believe"* (**John 4:48**).

God used these methods at home and abroad. Many people would have disregarded the gospel for some form of frightening divine intervention in their affairs. I had the opportunity to spend two hours with a state governor of Lagos in 2002. The meetings took place at an event that shook one of the most populous states in Nigeria. How did it happen?

It is my practice to intercede for this nation regularly. Our ministry partner was a top government official, and we usually prayed for the country and nations. During one of the intercessory sessions, the Lord spoke through me through the Spirit of prophecy about an imminent bomb blast.

The Lord told us a bomb blast was imminent in the state. The bomb blast exploded precisely four months later. Incidentally, this ministry partner forgot to bring the prophetic word to the attention of the state's leadership due to a culmination of events.

DIVINE PROMOTION

During another prayer session, a prophetic word came concerning this same ministry partner. The Spirit of the Lord said she would be made the director general at the federal level of government. That was in August 1998. Judging by human standards, such an accelerated promotion appeared unrealistic. When the prophetic word came, she was just a board member at the state level and nothing with federal service. True to the prophetic declaration, she was appointed a director general by the federal government in December 2001.

Nevertheless, she took opportunities to share her testimony with authority. When the bomb blast destroyed the place, she told the state/federal authorities that a prophet had predicted the incident.

Eventually, the state governor invited me to pray for the state. The opportunity came from prophetic utterances opening the doors of evangelism in high places. The Spirit of prophecy has come into operation even in strange places. God has declared deep things concerning men and women when I find myself outside my prayer closet.

EVANGELISTIC

In another instance, I was at a book launch in 1999. It turned out to be a forum where top political leaders met. The Spirit of the Lord spoke to me, and I told my host, "The Lord just told me now that a retired general will become the next president of Nigeria." I went further to tell her that he would be elected to serve two terms. Even though I was declaring the word of God, nobody in that country ever thought such a thing could happen.

The fellow later called to tell me that a retired general, Obasanjo, was sworn in as a civilian president in May 2000. She was stunned by exactly what the Spirit of the Lord had declared. She arranged for me to meet the new president. Again, I had the opportunity to share God's word with him through prophetic utterance. This kind of prophetic evangelism has become a regular occurrence in our ministry.

OPEN DOORS

As a tool, prophetic utterances open doors of opportunities. When you operate in the prophetic ministry and move into that realm, men and women will be ready to surrender their lives to Christ. Ordinary folks, hard-core unbelievers, and people who otherwise would never have considered the call to salvation will yield their lives to the Lord. Also, note you don't have to be a prophet to win souls.

Friends, the Bible states there is joy in heaven over every soul who repents; it clearly shows that evangelism is God's heartbeat. It means much to Him. He also affirms that any righteous believer involved with evangelism shall receive great rewards.

In my personal experience, I have noticed and received great favor through evangelism. God generally releases abundant grace to those addicted to evangelism. So, if you are ready to see that door open quickly, please shine your light wherever you find any opportunity to share the gospel.

Trust me, God's power will move by His Spirit. In return, God's supernatural power will open doors of blessing due to involvement in soul-winning. Just that encounter will transform your life.

Six

Fasting

Fasting is another potent tool for supernatural breakthroughs. My life is a living testimony and a powerful demonstration of the efficacy of fasting. Jesus said, *"And when you fast" (Matt. 6:16a)*, which translates that fasting is an essential ingredient of Christian living.

In this chapter, we shall examine the principles of scriptural fasting. Fasting is a vital tool that opens heaven. I believe in fasting, and I implore every Christian to ask for the grace to fast as needed.

Fasting hastens the fulfillment of the promises of God, unlocks every closed door, lightens every heavy burden, breaks every resistant yoke, and demonstrates the almightiness of God. Fasting takes the ordinary to the extraordinary realm, makes God's supernatural power available in every natural situation, and releases God's supernatural anointing, which breaks every yoke. God moves each time you fast, your spiritual life becomes sharper, and you will begin to receive uncommon favor from God and man.

Paul and Barnabas unlocked the plan of God for their life through fasting. "While they were worshiping the Lord and fasting, the Holy Spirit said, *'Set apart for me Barnabas and Saul* *for the work to which I have called them'" (**Acts 13:2**).* These two men discovered the work the Holy Spirit had appointed them to do and where to preach the gospel through the instrumentality of fasting.

Fasting is a tool that allows one to generate power to fulfill one's calling through the guidance of the Holy Spirit. *"Then Jesus was led up by the Spirit into the wilderness to be tempted by the devil. And after fasting forty days and forty nights, he was hungry" (**Matt. 4:1–2**).* Luke's account says, *"And Jesus returned in the power of the Spirit to Galilee" (*Luke 4:14*).* The anointing of divine ease will envelop your life when you begin to live a fasting life. When you become addicted, you will experience multiple supernatural breakthroughs. For example, you can see after Christ ended His fasting, He returned with power:

God taught me many lessons through the school of fasting. Out of these lessons, three stand out.

1. Purpose: Each time you fast, your purpose must be well-defined. Some people fast and need a definite goal. Purposeful fasting yields substantial results. Daniel 9:3 is a clear example of what Daniel did: "Then I turned my face to the Lord God, seeking him by prayer and pleas for mercy with fasting and sackcloth and ashes."

2. Devotion: Fasting helps us stay devoted, characterized by unfettered commitment. We must manifest absolute focus to remain in God's presence as we fast.

3. Listening: The essence of fasting is to find a solution to a need. However, fasting without prayer and listening to God's Spirit amounts to a hunger strike. Suppose you have decided to set some time apart for fasting. In that case, you must convert every moment to the guidance of the Holy Spirit to achieve maximum results.

THE FAST LANE

A common saying is, "If you fast, you will be in the fast lane." Indeed, the supernatural did not manifest in Jesus's ministry until He fasted. Fasting brings higher authority and spiritual sensitivity.

Fasting can rebuild and improve your relationship with God. Ancient Christians found that fasting aided them in regaining their first love for God. Also, it was, and remains, a way to stay humble in the sight of God. King David said, "When I wept and humbled my soul with fasting, it became my reproach" *(Ps. 69:10)*.

In 1998, I observed twenty-one days of fasting and prayer. At the end of the fast, I was passionate about praying for the sick, just as Christ commanded us to do: *"Now God anointed Jesus of Nazareth with the Holy Spirit and with power. He went about doing good and healing all who were oppressed by the devil, for God was with him" (Acts 10:38)*. I met a young man who was deaf.

I prayed with him, and he became healed. I have witnessed similar events over and over again to the glory of God the Father.

THE BELIEVER'S VOCATION

My beloved, God's gifts are sharpened by fasting and effective administration. Plus, they are more potent when mixed with faith. Fasting does not have to be long, but it is good to fast as a Christian. If Jesus did it as the Son of God, we are obliged to do the same. Most great preachers affirm fasting as a vital strength of their ministry. They attribute their success in the church to fasting.

TYPES OF FASTING

Esther Fast: Esther fasted to avert the extermination of the Jews. It was a three-day fast. It was a group fast without eating and drinking (Esther 4:15–17).

Samuel Fast: The prophet instructed the Israelites to fast for repentance and put away idols and strange gods (1 Sam. 7).

Elijah Fast: It was a forty-day fast, prompted by Jezebel's threat to kill him in revenge for killing four hundred of Baal's prophets, which frightened Elijah (***1 Kings 19:4–8***).

Ezra Fast: This was for God's intervention in resolving issues and for defense against the devil. The people fasted and prayed, and God gave them their wish (***Ezra 8:21–23***).

Daniel Fast: Daniel fasted for good health and to pursue God's blessing, purpose, and vision for his life (***Dan. 1:5-21, 10:3***).

John the Baptist Fast: This type of fast is to improve both our walk with God and our witness (***Luke 1:15***).

Jesus Fast: This type of fast is for spiritual strength and victory over temptation, flesh, and demons (***Matt. 4:1–2***).

HOW TO FAST

Normal Fast: No food, water only.

Partial Fast: This could mean fasting certain meals of the day or abstaining from certain foods (***Dan. 10:3***).

Absolute Fast: Absolutely no food or water, but it should not be over three days. Also, ensure there is the help of the Holy Spirit.

Fasting is a vital tool that opens heaven. It accelerates the realization of God's promises, opens closed doors, eases every heavy load, breaks every repellent yoke, and expresses the almightiness of God.

Paul and Barnabas unlocked the plan of God for their life through fasting, which means we generate power to fulfill God's calling through the guidance of the Holy Spirit.

We could see when Jesus fasted, He returned in the power of the Spirit to Galilee (Luke 4:14). The anointing of divine help will envelop our life when we begin fasting, and we will experience multiple supernatural breakthroughs. At the same time, we will gain power and spiritual sensitivity to rebuild and improve our bonding with God. Ancient Christians found that fasting helped them regain their first love for God. I can attest to this after twenty-one days of fasting. Truthfully, let us fast with a clear purpose, devotion, and listening to the guidance of the Holy Spirit, observing any fast that fits our situation.

All fasting should be observed based on individual personal conviction and medical advice from a physician.

SEVEN

GIVING

A popular saying is "Givers never lack." It is a true statement. Act 20:35 says, *"It is more blessed to give than to receive."* A typical example is Jesus's observation of a widow's gift:

And he sat down opposite the treasury and watched the people putting money into the offering box. Many rich people put in large sums. And a poor widow came and put in two small copper coins, which make a penny. And he called his disciples to him and said to them, "Truly, I say to you, this poor widow has put in more than all those who are contributing to the offering box. For they all contributed out of their abundance, but she, out of her poverty, has put in everything she had, all she had to live on." **Mark 12:41–44**

The act of giving opens doors of breakthroughs very fast, especially when you face any severe financial predicament. How can giving be used as a key that opens heaven? I will provide examples of a few people who have used giving to unlock the doors of their breakthroughs, as well as the various types of giving that can open the heavens.

ACCEPTABLE SACRIFICE

In Genesis 4, Cain and Abel offered a yearly sacrifice unto God. God had respect for Abel's offering because he gave it from the best of his flock and with a good heart. But Cain gave out the remnant of his farm. The heaven opened unto Abel and consumed the offering [J] because he gave cheerfully.

In 2 Chronicles 1:6, Solomon offered a thousand burnt offerings unto God. The same night, the Lord appeared unto him and gave him a blank check to ask for whatever he wanted in life. We all know Solomon was one of the wealthiest kings who had ever lived, and his testimony still blesses many today.

THE GLORIOUS LIFESTYLE

When Abraham sacrificed Isaac to God, the heavens opened and poured blessings upon him (Gen. 22:16). Today, we are all sons and daughters of Abraham. Giving brings us abundance. If we want fulfillment in life and ministry, we must embrace giving as a lifestyle.

Here are various types of giving that can unlock heaven: firstfruits, tithes, and sacrificial offerings.

1. *Firstfruits*

Many Christians do not know the importance of this offering, and many are unaware because they do not know. The firstfruits offering is the first blessing that God gives us: *"That thou shall set apart unto the lord all that openeth the matrix (womb) and every firstling that cometh of a beast which thou has the males shall be the lord"* (**Exod. 13:12**).

The giving of the firstfruits may be a hard thing to do, but the blessing is tremendous. Why did God bless Abraham? It was not because he paid his tithe in Genesis 14 but because he observed the ordinances of the firstfruits offering.

THE MYSTERY OF INCREASE

The Bible says, *"And it came to pass after these things, After these things God tested Abraham and said to him"* (Gen. 22:1). God tested Abraham to see if he would obey the ordinance of offering Isaac as firstfruits. In this scripture, Abraham was obedient, and God made a promise to him: *"I will surely bless you, and I will surely multiply your offspring as the stars of heaven and as the sand that is on the seashore. And your offspring shall possess the gate of his"* (Gen. 22:17).

First, the Bible promised that fruit offers an increase of multiplication of thirty, sixty, and hundredfold. It also enhances victory over the enemies, as God promised. The promise of being blessed thirty, sixty, and hundredfold can be retrieved when we observe the ordinance of the firstfruits offering.

If we sow on good ground in good faith, the law of multiplication cannot elude us. *"But those that were sown on the good soil are the ones who hear the word and accept it and bear fruit, thirtyfold and sixtyfold and a hundredfold" (Mark 4:20).*

2. Tithe

This is one-tenth of the resources we give after giving our fruit in the first month. Tithes serve as an insurance policy in the kingdom. After Abraham paid tithes to Melchizedek in Genesis 14, the Lord told Abraham, *"Fear not, Abram, I am your shield; your reward shall be very great" (Gen. 15:1).* Tithes also prevent devourers from attacking us, according to Malachi 3. That is just the importance of tithes. However, it is a choice.

3. Sacrificial Offering

This is a willing offering we give as God leads. In **Malachi 3,** the Bible commands us to bring offerings into His storehouse. The sacrificial offering can be classified in three ways:

a. *Kingdom offering:* We give these offerings to God's projects (e.g., churches and temples). In Genesis 25:2, the Lord told Moses to command the children of Israel to give Him a willing offering to build His sanctuary. As they obeyed the Lord, He blessed them. Other examples include offerings by David and Solomon (see 1 Chronicles 28 and 2 Chronicles 2).

b. *Prophetic offering:* These are offerings we give to men of God. This offering stirs up anointing. In 1 Samuel 9, Saul offered a prophetic offering unto Samuel, and Solomon then received the anointing that brought him into the limelight as a king. So, if we desire God's blessing, we must sow a seed into a prophet's life. We will then see our desires granted.

c. *Needy offering:* These are offerings to assist the widows, the needy, and the orphans. It was the secret of the most incredible man in the East (Job 29:1–16). If we practice this giving, the heavens will open for us in all areas of our lives. We will surely experience supernatural breakthroughs.

4. ***Thanksgiving Offering***

God always demands thanksgiving from us. Psalm 92 says, *"It is good to give thanks to the Lord, to sing praises to your name, O Most High."* Also, 1 Thessalonians 5:18a says, *"Give thanks in all circumstances; for this is the will of God in Christ Jesus for you."* Be grateful to God and be blessed. If we are givers, we will continue to receive supernatural breakthroughs.

Giving opens doors of breakthroughs very fast, especially when facing any severe financial predicament. How can giving be used as a key that opens heaven? I will provide examples of a few people who use giving to unlock the doors of their breakthroughs, and the various types of giving that can open the heavens.

But there are sacrifices God honors, like Abel, Abraham, and Solomon's gifts, because they came from obedience and a willing heart; the heavens opened and granted their requests. Also, we can give God various kinds of offerings to move His hands, like firstfruits, tithes, sacrificial offerings, prophetic offerings, welfare offerings, and thanksgiving offerings to unlock the blessings of God. Friends, apply the key of giving, and favor will come your way.

Conclusion

In all folks, keys grant us access to houses, cars, gates, and safes. Keys come in different shapes. Imagine a bunch of keys to a building. The first thing that comes to mind is to figure out the keys that open various doors and the safe. The gates of heaven are closed; we must apply the right key to gain access. Friends, we need to know how to use these keys—the Word, thanksgiving, praise, prayer, fasting, giving, and evangelism—as tools to unlock the gates of heaven.

Since God created everything through the instrumentality of His Word, His Word is utmost in all facets of our life. God's Word is the master key and the requirement to receive anything. But our results become more evident as we get intimate with the Holy Spirit.

We must deal with God with a grateful heart and stop grumbling. Paul implores us to be thankful in all situations. God takes delight in our praises; He wants us to rejoice, serve, sing, and bless His name. When we do that, we draw power from heaven. Praise gladdens God's heart and makes the devil mad. Moses and the children of Israel understood the power of praise; it brought down His presence in the wilderness. David and Deborah used the same weapon of praise to defeat the devil.

Besides praise or thanksgiving, prayer is another strategic key that Jesus taught His disciples. Also, Jonah, Elijah, and Daniel prayed through the leading of the Spirit. God will answer prayer if we follow the rudiments of prayer. He is not a respecter of man but of those who obey His law.

More so, God gets fascinated when we evangelize; it is God's heartbeat. And if we want a breakthrough, we must do what pleases Him. It is then we will see our light shining.

On the other hand, we must uphold the key of fasting. It opens closed doors, breaks yokes, and expresses the invincibility of God. It unlocks God's plan for our life, just as it did for Paul and Barnabas when they fasted. Also, we generate power to fulfill our mission when we fast, just as Jesus did, and return in the Spirit's power. Let us fast and see God's anointing flow into our lives.

Finally, we must practice the act of giving. It opens doors to breakthroughs, especially when faced with financial difficulty. We must practice giving that meets God's standards, like Abel, Abraham, and Solomon's. Above all, we must use these keys rightly, master them, continue to build up ourselves, and believe in God so that He shall grant all our requests. Shalom!

Made in the USA
Coppell, TX
27 October 2024

38872791R00038